التنوع بالنسبة لي

By Marisa J. Taylor
Illustrated by Fernanda Monteiro

BILINGUAL
English - Arabic

التنوع بالنسبة لي
Diversity to me

Text & Illustration Copyright © 2022 by Lingobabies

Written by Marisa Taylor

Illustrated by Fernanda Monteiro

ISBN: 978-1-914605-46-8 (paperback)
ISBN: 978-1-914605-49-9 (hardcover)

Edited by Shari Last
Arabic Translation by Kholoud Ahmed
Graphic Design by Sohail Sikandar

All rights reserved. This book or any portion thereof may not be reproduced or used in any manner without the permission of the publisher except for the use of brief quotations in a book review.

This book is dedicated to all the children of the world who feel insecure about their differences. May you learn to love and embrace what makes you different from the rest.

Every day tell yourself one thing you love about yourself and always remember that you are perfect just the way you are.

This book is also dedicated to my children, who I love dearly. You inspire me to be a better person and to use my voice to stand up against racism & inequalities.

هذا الكتاب مخصص لجميع أطفال العالم الذين يشعرون بعدم الأمان تجاه اختلافاتهم. قد تتعلم أن تحب وتتقبل ما يجعلك مخلفا عن الآخرين.

أخبر نفسك كل يوم بشيء واحد تحبه في نفسك وتذكر دائمًا أنك مثالي تمامًا كما أنت .

هذا الكتاب مخصص أيضًا لأطفالي الذين أحبهم كثيرًا. أنتم تلهمونني لأكون شخصًا أفضل وأن أستخدم صوتي للوقوف ضد العنصرية وعدم المساواة.

Marisa Taylor

Hi, what's your name?

مرحبا ما اسمك؟

....

Do you know the word, "diversity"?
Let me tell you what that word means to me.

هل تعرف كلمة "التنوع"؟
دعني أخبرك ماذا تعني هذه الكلمة بالنسبة لي.

Diversity is about being different:
A different look, a different culture, a different race.
A different ethnicity - even a different face.

التنوع هو أن تكون مختلفًا:
مظهر مختلف، ثقافة مختلفة، جنس مختلف
عرق مختلف - حتى وجه مختلف..

Because if everyone was born the same, the world would be boring.

لأنه لو ولد الجميع متشابهين، لكان العالم مملاً.

أحب كلمة "مختلف". تجعلني أشعر بالحرية تذكرني أنه لا يوجد أحد متطابق معي. هناك نسخة واحدة مني أنا. أنا واحدة فقط.

I have curly hair, brown skin,
and freckles on my face.
But that's not what defines me.
It's my joy and style and grace.

لدي شعر مجعد وبشرة بنية اللون ونمش على وجهي لكن هذا ليس ما يميزني. إنها فرحتي وأسلوبي وامتناني.

My friend Ore is different, too:
he is not like me.
He is shy and quiet - the
kindest kid you'll ever see.

صديقي أور مختلف أيضًا. فهو لا يشهني إنه خجول وهادئ، وهو ألطف طفل يمكن أن تراه على الإطلاق.

Alexia is different, too.
She loves to paint and run.
She's the fastest kid I know.
Together we have such fun!

أليكسيا مختلفة أيضًا. تحب الرسم والجري.
إنها أسرع طفلة أعرفها معًا نحظى بمثل هذا المرح!

My friend Noah is an artist - he's definitely unique.
He's also such a joker,
I laugh each time we speak.

صديقي نوح فنان ـ إنه بالتأكيد فريد من نوعه. وهو أيضًا شخص يحب المزاح، أضحك في كل مرة نتحدث فيها.

We all are beautiful!
We have special powers to offer the world,
and that is our story.

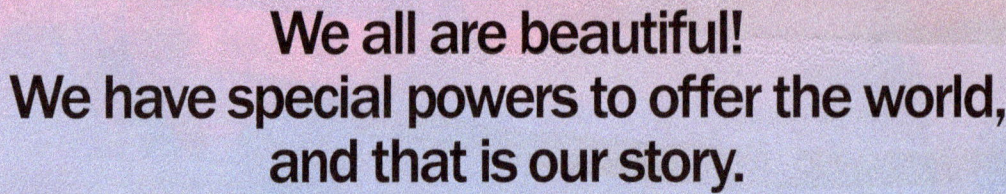

كلنا جميلون! لدينا قوى خاصة لكي نقدمها للعالم، وهذه هي قصتنا.

We should never judge someone for who they are, but accept them in all their glory.

لا ينبغي لنا أبدًا أن نحكم على شخص ما بسبب هويته، لكن نقبلهم بكل مجدهم.

Our physical, cultural, and religious differences make the world a beautiful place.

إن اختلافاتنا الجسدية والثقافية والدينية تجعل العالم مكاناً جميلاً.

Differences are beautiful,
and are there for us to embrace.

الاختلافات جميلة، وهي موجودة لكي نتقبلها.

Everyone has their own special talents. That's what makes us shine - you and me.
And that is the true beauty of diversity.

كل شخص لديه مواهبه الخاصة. وهذا يجعلنا نتألق - أنت وأنا. وهذا هو الجمال الحقيقي للتنوع.

ماذا يعني لك التنوع؟

About the creators

Marisa Taylor is a German/Canadian Author who resides in London, UK with her husband and children. They are a multiracial & multilingual family. Marisa has always been interested in learning & teaching languages, as she feels that it is the key element to connecting with people from other cultures. After becoming a mother she saw the lack of diverse resources available and became passionate about creating diverse bilingual resources that encourage children to celebrate multiculturalism and to learn a second language.

Instagram: @lingobabies

Fernanda Monteiro is a Brazilian illustrator and a mother of two, Íris and Aurora. She graduated in journalism, but her dream was always to work with drawing and found that the best way to do this would be through creating illustrations for children's books. Fernanda believes that through art she can contribute towards a better world in the future.

Instagram: @fe.monteiro_art

www.ingramcontent.com/pod-product-compliance
Lightning Source LLC
Chambersburg PA
CBHW041216240426
43661CB00012B/1064